# *Introduction*

My name is Herman Muhammad and I am a
self described 21st Century Renaissance
Man, I am a young entrepreneur who through
hard work and dedication has been able to
make a substantial amount of money doing
what I love, barbering.

This little book is a guide or formula to achieve
success in this particular field. However, the
principles that we will discuss can be used in
just about any entrepreneurial endeavor.

This book is a collection of the many
anecdotes and lessons that I have learned
and lived in the 15 years that I have been in
business. I hope that it is helpful.

1

# Love

I have always prided myself as being a very uncomplicated guy so I intend to make this book and the principles within as simple as possible. With that said, the first step to getting rich in the Barbering industry is knowing how to cut hair and to love it!

Now that may seem like an over simplified first step but I assure you it is not. In fact, it is vitally necessary. As stated before the steps outlined in this book will not only be applicable to barbering and cosmetology but to any entrepreneurial endeavor.

In other words, to get rich in any business endeavor one has to truly love what he/she is doing. You have to truly love cutting and/or styling hair if you are to get rich in the barbering/cosmetology industry.

Think about it. If you are going to do something full time should not you at least enjoy that particular thing? There are so many people I come in contact with that absolutely hate their job yet they continue working because they get a paycheck. These people are stuck in a type of "Hell" because they are never truly fulfilled in their professional lives.

I know, it is a job and the bills have to be paid right? Yes they do have to be paid but at what price? You only have one life to live and a substantial percentage of that time is spent working. Let us break it down. There are 24 hours in a day...actually there are 23 hour, 56 minutes and 46 seconds to be exact but you get the point. Out of those 24 hours, eight of them are spent at work and it's really 9 or 10 hours when you consider transit to and from work as well as the time the average person spends getting ready for work.

In that same day you will spend 6 to 8 hours sleeping so that leaves close to 6 hours for you to spend eating dinner and enjoying time with the family. The point of all of this is that the majority of time in your average day will be taken by work.

The reality is that if you do not love your job or even like it, those negative feelings and energy will carry over into other areas of your life. Therefore, it would be wise if you loved what you do for a living.

The benefits of loving what you do will not be lost on your clients either. It will reflect in your work and they will be more than happy to compensate you and add a generous gratuity.

I was once taught by by my mentor that love and life were two words that were interchangeable. So if you think about it in that light, if you love what you do it will actually feed and enrich your life. That spirit and enthusiasm will be transferred to your clients through the service that you provide and all will be affected positively!

Love your work and it won't be work at all and you will still get paid. Now is that great or what?

# Be Legit!

*Legit* is slang or ebonics for the the word *legitimate* in case you did not know. The simplest definition for legitimate is 'to be in compliance with the law.' Get your barber or cosmetology license! Again, this may seem like an obvious point but I could not tell you how many illegitimate, boot-leg, basement, so-called barbers there are in my home state as well as the United States that are perpetrating a fraud at this very moment.

Barbering/cosmetology is an art as well as a profession so each state has set up rules and regulations to govern their practice. It is disrespectful to the profession to be practicing as a barber/cosmetologist without the proper license and/or certifications. It is also unethical and unsafe.

Consider this, barbering as well as a practice called bloodletting were both practiced one time in barbershops. Bloodletting was a practice employed by Barber Surgeons to cure illnesses and restore health and thrived as a practice in the 19th century. Barber Surgeons also would amputate limbs, pull teeth and perform other so-called minor surgeries. I point all this out to illustrate how well respected and honored the barbering profession was and is.

An illustration of bloodletting. The barber pole originated from the blood and the towels used to clean up.

As stated before, every state has procedures, guidelines and agencies in place that govern the practice of barbering and cosmetology. With this in mind you be a legitimate and lawful practitioner of this most honored profession. It will also aid you in establishing a professional reputation which you will need in order to get rich!

When I received my barber license it took around 1250 hours of class time plus an externship at a licensed shop to complete the requirements to apply for a license. Once completed I had to schedule a time to take the state exam which was two parts, written and practical and took two days to complete. All of these steps also required that you pay the necessary fees that accompanied the exam.

For cosmetologists the number of hours was 1450 plus the externship. I was licensed in the state of Colorado and I remember wondering if the number of hours required was excessive just to learn how to cut hair. But upon enrolling in the course I learned so much more than just cutting hair. I learned that in order to be a barber or cosmetologist that you needed to learn the anatomy and chemical composition of hair as well as sanitization and sterilization.

We learned the state laws that governed our industry as well as professionalism and basic business skills that would prove to be priceless upon entrance in the field.

7

We learned that people trust their barber/ cosmetologist more than they trust their doctors or other professionals. And we learned that barbering and cosmetology have a rich historical tradition that should be honored. For instance, Madame C.J. Walker was the first black female millionaire in this country and she happened to be a cosmetologist.

Would you go to a doctor, lawyer, counselor or even an auto mechanic if they were not licensed or certified in their profession? I know for a fact that I would not so why should not the public expect the same level of professionalism from their barber or cosmetologist?

Practicing barbering or cosmetology without a license is as stated before, perpetrating a fraud and there are serious legal consequences for doing so. Usually it is in the form of fine and some kind of future sanction against you getting a license. But more importantly, to practice without a license speaks volumes about your own personal character. It means that you are willing to take a chance at doing something that you know is illegal for your own personal financial gain.

It means that you have yet to grow into a person who has integrity. And it means that you are not really serious about being a professional barber or cosmetologist. Furthermore, it means that you do not really desire to become rich or successful in this profession.

Get the proper license and certification and you will be well on your way to becoming whatever you want to be in this profession. I cannot stress this enough. There are a multitude of options you will have in terms of your career in the hair industry. The only way you will able to take advantage of all the opportunities though is to have the proper credentials.

You can be a platform artist, barber, cosmetologist, product representative, hair colorist, shop owner or anything you desire if you take the proper steps. It is entirely up to you. Be legit that is it and the possibilities are endless. Remember these principles apply to any and every field of endeavor.

# My Mentor

I felt compelled to add this chapter because like all the other steps involved in being successful and getting rich it is vitally important. A mentor in the simplest terms is a person who is what and where you eventually want to be in life. He or she would be a template for your business life.

Now I am not suggesting that in every aspect of life that they are exactly what you want to be. But they should at least come close if they are to be a true mentor. It would be good if they are in the same profession but does not have to be the case. They need to have a work ethic that you desire to emulate and the willingness to share their wisdom with you.

Some of us are so arrogant that we think no one can teach us anything. We have such a sense of independence that we want to be considered leaderless and we want everyone to recognize that we are successful only because of "me." This is a foolish way to think because the moment that we think we know it all, we stop growing. And anything that is not growing is either stagnant or dead.

Consider this, Solomon said "there is nothing new under the sun" and that is a prolific and wise statement. Human Beings have been on this planet for millions of years and have conducted business the whole time. You have been on this Earth for a relatively short period of time in comparison.

This means that there are people who have done things already that you desire to do. There are people that have a wealth of experience that could be helpful to you in your life journey. In short, there are people who can lead you. You just have to be willing to accept their leadership.

A mentor is a leader who will help you get where you desire to be. He or she should be able to give you tidbits of wisdom that will help you. They are a valued resource for your personal and professional life. I personally have had at least three mentors that have helped me in my journey and I am still traveling.

All of my mentors are spiritually, mentally, professionally and practically wise. I would not have it any other way. They have helped me in ways that they do not even know and I am eternally grateful.

Mentorship is important in your journey because it hopefully will carry on and over through you mentoring someone else. Each one, teach one comes to mind because everyone has something to offer or teach. There is not a person alive who does not have a life lesson that does not contain value for someone else.

With all these things in mind, find a suitable mentor(s) and follow their advice. When you are ready you should mentor someone else with exacting care so that they may be as successful as you and the circle of reciprocity can continue.

A principle I learned a long time ago comes to mind, "one cannot be a good leader until they are a good follower." So that same principle applies to being a good mentor. Keep that in mind and you will be held in high regard by a whomever you mentor and all that observe your mentorship.

# Branding

Branding is a term that is used in business marketing and is extremely important in establishing your business as a barber or cosmetologist. In this business **YOU** are your greatest commodity or product! Branding is the method by which you will get your product (you) out to the consumer.

Now you may not think that this concept applies to you but I assure you that it does. The sooner you learn and accept it the better, for it will allow you to do so much better in your pursuit of becoming rich in this game.

Your brand is what makes you stand out from everyone else that is in your industry. For instance, McDonalds comes to mind when I think of companies with instant brand recognition. Where ever you see those "golden arches" you know there is a cheeseburger and fries somewhere ready to be eaten.

I does not matter whether the food even tastes good and personally I do not think that it does. It only matters that you recognize the brand, know what you are getting and buy accordingly. So McDonalds is one of the most instantly recognized companies in the world.

Now I know you are not selling burgers but the principle is what I am trying to point out. You want your name to be branded onto the minds of your potential clients and associated with the service that you provide. Just like McDonalds is synonymous with burgers you want your name to be synonymous with barbering or cosmetology.

To achieve this goal there are a number of things that you will have to do. First you have to be proficient at what you do in regards to cutting and/or styling hair. Your proficiency should not only be recognized by you but by your clients as well as your peers in the industry. To be clearer, people should compliment you on your skill set and recommend you to other clients. The greatest form of advertising in this business is word of mouth so people should have your name in their mouths in regards to barbering or cosmetology.

Next you should develop your personal business acumen. This means that you should be to work on time, provide excellent service at a fair price and exemplify the utmost professionalism at all times. Alway remember that you are not selling burgers you are selling a service. In short, you are selling yourself!

Another indicator of one's professionalism is a business card. Again, this may seem obvious but I cannot tell you how many times I have encountered a barber or stylist and asked them for a card and received a puzzling look. Or they give you the old "I just ran out" excuse. The bottom line is that you are trying to establish yourself in the business world. Therefore you have to have a business card in order to be taken seriously as a business person.

Another aspect of branding or marketing is social and internet marketing. This is vitally important if you desire to be visible in the ever-changing market of today. The most powerful thing about using social media as a marketing/branding tool is that it is free! It will take absolutely nothing from your advertising budget.

Sites like Facebook and Twitter have changed the way that companies brand themselves. Now you cannot even be in business if you do not have an online presence and engage in social networking. Use these sites to your advantage by posting pictures of your work as well as promotions that you will run.

You should also build a website that features your work and promotes your brand. Websites can range in price from being very expensive to being totally free! Search engines like Yahoo! and Google will actually provide free sites. You simply sign up, follow the set-up instructions and enter your content.

When deciding how to brand yourself you should try to keep your ideas simple, elegant and memorable. Focus on your particular skill set. If you do razor fades really well, hair weaves or razor cuts then you should advertise that as a specialty.

The idea is to become known for a particular skill thereby becoming reputable. Always remember, in this industry you can advertise as much as you like but the the best form of advertising is word of mouth. You want your clients to talk positively to their friends, family and associates encouraging them to patronize you. Your clientele will increase and your skills will become synonymous with your brand.

Other forms of marketing include flyers, newspaper ads, coupons, etc. The important thing is that you be imaginative and innovative in the way that you advertise your business. Be cautious when running specials. As a matter of fact, I rarely discount my services because you don't want to make a bad habit of de-valuing what you do. Remember, YOU are your greatest commodity!

One more thing on branding, Sprite which is a Coca Cola product used to have an ad that stated *"Image is Everything, Obey Your Thirst!"* I would like to focus on the first part, image. Image is such an interesting thing because it is the first thing that people see. I always liked that ad because it contains a proven truth.

Image is everything because oftentimes people judge with their most basic of senses, sight. With this in mind you should have a clean and respectable image as you establish self and brand. Everything about you and the skills that you are advertising should present an impeccable, polished image.

It is interesting because we live in a time when tattoos and piercing are all the rage and style. But with that being said, as an employer, I would never hire a barber or stylist who had a tattoo on their face. To me, that does not look professional nor does it represent the image that I want reflected in my business. You might find some that will hire persons like that but not many.

A large part of the barbering and cosmetology industry has to do with sterilization and sanitation. Barbers and cosmetologists should be clean in appearance as well as demeanor. In establishing your brand you should emphasize knowledge in this area. Remember, people are coming to you so you can make them look good. You should look good too!

This is my logo, my brand and the image I want engrained in peoples' minds when they think of barbering.

# Hustle!

I'm a hustler! Straight up! Excuse my ghetto vernacular but I have to speak straight words that get to the point. I say hustle because the word implies a need to get something done quickly for a sizable profit or reward.

Another reason I use that word is because a lot of times we come from a world where hustling is familiar. We simply want to make the transition from "street hustling" to legitimate business dealings. The principles remain largely the same.

A person who used to hustle illegally in the streets knows how to make money, plain and simple. Now as a barber or cosmetologist, we simply apply those same principles of getting money to our new profession.

We have already discussed being legitimate and branding in previous chapters and they both correlate with the topic at hand in this chapter. Hustling is the act of getting people to come and sit in your chair to enjoy the benefit of your services in exchange for money.

To truly be a hustler you need to draw on everything that has been discussed in previous chapters and then manifest it in the way that will draw people into your chair/business. You have to make yourself into a magnet for potential clients. Remember this is a numbers business and the more clients you have, the more likely it is that you will become rich.

Being in this business for as long as I have there are tremendous lessons that I have learned. One such lesson is the fact that the true essence of business is not about money. Money is the draw that attracts most people but business is really about relationships. This is especially true in the practice of barbering and cosmetology.

*Business is the practice of making one's living by engaging in commerce,* according to the dictionary but what I speak of is the essence of business, relationships.
Relationships are exactly what the word implies, how we get along or relate to others.

How are relationships more important to money in business? It is simple, every successful business has a relationship with their customers. There is a comfort level within that relationship whether it be the customer just relating to the culture of that particular business or something more personal.

As a business person you should not just be interested in just making a quick buck. Instead you should focus on the long term influx of dollars coming by way of your well pleased clients with whom you have established good relationships.

Relationships are key because they will determine whether you have longevity in this business or whether you will be looking for a new career sooner than later. Historically barbers and cosmetologists have thrived in even the most difficult times. It is because of these facts that you should concentrate on this particular aspect of your business.

As a hustler, we have to be loved or at least liked by those that patronize us. As mentioned in previous chapters the relationship between barber/cosmetologist and client can be considered as important or more so than a doctor/patient relationship to many. This should encourage us to foster good relationships with our clients because that will certainly endear them to you causing more money to flow from their hand to you pockets.

I mentioned that barbers and cosmetologists historically have thrived in the most trying of economic times. This is because the field is considered by many to be recession proof. To put it simply, people come to get their hair done because they want to look good and because it is psychologically beneficial. If times are good, people want to look and feel good. Likewise, if things are bad, people still want to look and feel good!

If you have established relationships with you clients then they will patronize you consistently whether economic times are good or bad. You may see business taper off a little during the bad times but those clients will most likely resume their personal grooming regimen when things get better.

As you develop your marketing strategy and continue on your hustle you will find that there are times during the year that are really busy

24

and times when things slow down a bit. This is also true in regards to your work week. Usually early on in the week things are slower and gradually pick up as you approach the weekend.

A true hustler will take note of these observations and plan accordingly. For instance, when it is slow that is the best time to get out and do some marketing or advertising. There is a common misconception among new barbers and cosmetologists that makes them to think that clients are "magically" going to come and jump into their chair after they acquire a position at a shop or salon. This is just not true. On rare occasions, one might become employed at a really busy salon where walk-ins are abundant thereby giving them the opportunity to win new clients fairly easily. But if this scenario is to happen than that barber/cosmetologist is extremely lucky and is the exception not the rule.

In my experience, when you see a barber or stylist that is always busy with clients and has fat pockets to prove it then that barber/cosmetologist has worked tirelessly for years to make that his/her reality. They have spent countless hours honing their skills and developing relationships with their beloved clients. In essence, they know how to hustle. They know all of the tricks of the trade that win people to their chair and they have the ability and professionalism that keeps clients coming back.

A hustler is a worker. He or she is constantly training and conditioning his or herself to meet and overcome all obstacles that lay in their professional paths. So when business is slow, put out some flyers or tweet or post pictures or specials via your social networking accounts.

When you are picking up supplies or grocery shopping, strike up conversations with potential clients and hand out business cards. And when it is busy at the shop or salon, service your clients with the utmost professionalism never taking their patronage for granted. With every excellent service that you provide to your clients, your hustle will be further solidified.

Barber Sayeed Malik getting his "hustle" on.....supreme....

Another thing we have to keep in mind is that no matter how tempting it is, NEVER allow anything illegal to come into your business. I don't care if it's selling bootleg movies or other illegally obtained merchandise. As a barber or cosmetologist the only thing you want to sell is haircuts, hairstyles and other related products that have been legally obtained. Do not ever give the authorities reason to come in and destroy everything you have worked to build just to make a quick buck. If you want to be the neighborhood criminal or wannabe kingpin, then be that and leave the barbering and cosmetology to the professionals.

# Be Business

This like previous chapters is extremely important! When I say "be business" I am referring to the way we handle our money. How we for it, how we spend it and overall, how we view it.

Barbers and cosmetologists particularly in the African American community are in a unique and powerful position because we deal for the most part in a cash business. This makes us very valuable assets to our community because we are small businesses that provide employment to members of our community where there are not too many like us in other industries.

The black barber/cosmetologist is a well respected institution in our community so we have a responsibility to be the best business model that we can. In order to do this we must get our business ducks in a row. The first step is to keep accurate account of our money, both income and expenses.

29

As stated before, we deal in a mostly cash business so we have to be meticulous about the way that we account for our money. When you deal mostly in cash it is very easy if you are not careful to spend unwisely. For this reason barbers and cosmetologists have to limit the number of bad habits they have in order to be successful. You may ask, "what bad habits?"

When you have cash and in many cases cash is king then certain people will have the tendency to be the king as often as possible. They will spend as long as they have money just because they have it on the most frivolous things. These barbers and cosmetologists are what I refer to as "ghetto celebrities." They feel so good about making money doing for self that they foolishly trick it off! This can be done in the nightclub buying drinks or by chasing strange women or men.

Another vile habit which I consider the worst is excessive alcohol or drug consumption. I mentioned alcohol first because it is legally and socially acceptable thereby making it the most easily abused. It is real bad when you are a drunk and you have cash every day at your disposal. That makes one an accident on purpose waiting to happen.

It comes down to having discipline. As a business person who deals mostly with cash (if this is the case) you have to resist the urge to become a "ghetto celebrity." This means that you must have a business bank account that you make deposits into regularly. You should record every service that you perform in a ledger as well as what you charge for that particular service. You also want to keep every receipt that you receive for business expenditures.

This is essential for you being able to keep track of and grow your business. Most of us were never taught the "science" of business so we don't see the wisdom of these simple yet effective practices. Let's take them one by one:

1.  Get a business bank account and make deposits regularly. You want to do this because it will get you into the mentality of being a business person. I specified that it be a business account because that will ensure that you separate your business income/expenses from your own personal

financial information. You want to have a separation between the two for legal and tax purposes. Make deposits regularly so that you won't have cash in your pockets at all times ready to spend.

2.  Record every service and the amount charged in a ledger to keep track of how much money you are making. This will let you know how you are doing financially and enable you to do some life planning based upon your income. It will also help you determine when your busiest times are and when your slowest times are on a weekly and monthly basis.

3.  Keep track of all business expenditures by keeping all receipts. As a business person you have to keep track of all the money that you spend. This is important for tax purposes and it is a standard bookkeeping practice. This will give you a general idea of weekly and monthly expenses, thereby allowing you to devise a business budget and stick to it. You can purchase programs for your Mac or PC that will help you in these areas.

You will also need to find out what the tax laws are in regards to your business structure. Small businesses are usually structured in one of the following ways: a sole proprietorship, a partnership, a corporation or a limited liability corporation(LLC). You can check with your Secretary of State's office to find out which structure will be the most beneficial for your individual situation.

There are pros and cons to each business structure so as stated before make sure you contact your Secretary of State for information regarding this subject.

Once you decide what type of business structure you will use you will also need to get a Federal tax identification number. Having this is important because it will allow you to obtain the proper business banking accounts as well as commercial insurance policies in the event you become a shop owner. You'll also want to enlist the services of a good accountant or tax person. Don't be intimidated by this at all and don't think that you cannot afford an accountant. There are a large number of accountants whose prices are affordable for a small business like yours and well worth it.

If this seems overwhelming, rest assured, these things discussed in this little book are very easy to obtain. All you have to do is "Google" whatever you need and the computer will take you wherever you need to go.

You need to "be business" if you are to be in business and that is the bottom line. This will allow you to grow your business properly especially in the difficult economic climate of today. Furthermore, the more "business" you are the more likely you are to get rich!

**supreme style barbershop**

Herman Muhammad (Master Barber)

7520 E Colfax Ave Denver, CO 80220

303.322.6941 w 720.300.0206 c

muhammadherman@yahoo.com or facebook.com/HermanMuhammad

**www.astar2.com**

My business card, a must for any professional barber/ stylist.

# Tools

There is a saying among craftsmen that "you are only as good as your tools." I do not necessarily agree with that because I think that it is an inaccurate generalization. In my experience, if you are a good barber or cosmetologist then you will make magic with whatever tools you use.

With that being said, if you desire to be the best at whatever you do you need to have the very best tools to accomplish this. Those tools are both physical and mental. Of course the physical tools are comprised of all implements such as clippers and razors, flatirons, blow dryers, combs, brushes etc. that a barber or cosmetologist would use on a daily basis. Make sure that you invest in the very best professional equipment.

As far as barber clippers are concerned there are a number of manufacturers that make great clippers. The best of these in my humble and professional opinion are in no particular order, Andis, Oster and Wahl. All of these brands can be found at your local barber or beauty supply. They also can be found online usually at discounted prices, I might add.

As a professional barber or cosmetologist you are going to want to keep from purchasing any of your equipment from big box stores like Walmart or Target. It may look tempting to purchase from places like this because the prices are so comparatively low. But trust me, the reason the prices of these clipper sets at these places are so low is because the quality and durability of these particular products are substandard as far as professional barbering is concerned.

As a professional you will be running your clippers for eight hours a day and sometimes longer than that! For this reason alone, your tools need to be reliable and durable. You can normally tell the difference between professional clipper sets and Walmart/Target brands by the thickness of the cord. The professional set will have a nice, thick cord while the home clipper set will have a power cord that is less substantial.

This is good information to have because Walmart, Target, Kmart and even Walgreen's will sell Oster or Wahl brand home clipper sets. The difference between these and professional sets as stated before, can be seen in the thickness of the power cord. These home clipper sets also are different in regards to the weight of the clipper and slight differences in the blade sets.

Again, purchase your clipper sets from a professional barber or beauty supply and you will assuredly get the best quality tools for what you are trying to accomplish. Professional barber and beauty supply stores are the ones that you patronize that require a license in order for you to purchase at a discount. These places are open to the public but require a licensed barber or cosmetologist to purchase a membership or most times the membership is free. You just have to show your license and they will sign you right up.

Other implements that should be purchased and used regularly by the professional barber or cosmetologist include but are not limited to; shears, razors, combs, flat/curling irons, blow dryers, combs and brushes. My advice in regards to these is the same as my recommendation for purchasing clippers. Stay away from the big box stores and purchase only from professional suppliers.

A general rule to go by in this field is the more expensive you tools are the better they will perform. Now this is a generalization that is genuinely true in my experience, especially when it comes to haircutting shears. An expensive pair of shears will most likely last you a lifetime and normally be accompanied by a lifetime guarantee when purchased. On the other hand, an inexpensive pair will be replaced time and time again.

If you are to be successful in this industry, you have to look at your equipment as an investment into your own success. An investment is something that is going to bring a substantial return at some point in time. If you invest wisely you will see a return on your investment sooner than later.

So invest in a good pair of shears and you most definitely will see the return. If you have questions in regards to how much to spend on a good pair of shears, ask the salesperson at the supply store. They usually have good working knowledge of the products they sell.

You will find that once you are working in the field that you will develop preferences with respect to what tools and implements you favor most. You will also take a liking to certain brands over others. Just work with the tools that work best for you and work with the tools that make your clients pleased with your work.

Another aspect of this tool piece is maintenance. You will have to maintain your tools and equipment to get the most out of them. You should always follow the manufacturers instructions on how to best use and maintain your tools. After all, who knows best how to maintain a product more than the one who manufactured it?

A professional barber or cosmetologist should keep all tools and implements as clean, sanitized and sterilized as possible. Clippers and trimmers should be sanitized and oiled according to the manufactures instruction. Shears and blades should be cleaned, oiled and sharpened according to manufacturers instruction as well. If you have good tools that are maintained properly those tools can last you forever.

Just as important as your physical tools are the mental "tools" that you bring to the table. Your mindset and attitude will play a major roll in your success as a barber or cosmetologist. There is an old saying that states, "your attitude determines your altitude." That is to say that the way you think towards any given situation will determine how far up you will go in life. I find this to be a profound and prolific statement.

A positive attitude will take you very, very far as opposed to a negative one. People do not want to be around a person with a negative attitude nor do they want to get their hair cut by that type of person. So in this profession, a positive attitude will be the most effective "mental tool" that you can possess.

This like many other concepts in this little book may seem obvious to some but you would be surprised at how many people do not realize how important a positive attitude is. The first step in accomplishing any goal is to fashion that particular idea in your mind. You cannot fashion an idea in your mind without thinking positively about it.

Another mental tool that will help you on your journey to success in this business will be your ability to establish good relationships with your clients. To be more specific, you will need to develop a good memory. Some people are born with a good memory but others have to develop theirs.

What does your memory have to do with establishing good relationships? Well just think about it  there is an old saying that states, "there is nothing sweeter in the ear of a person than the sound of his/her name." This means people love to be recognized and appreciated by those whom they patronize.

It makes all the difference in the world how a person feels when they walk into your shop or salon and you call them by their name. It shows that your relationship is not only business but that you care about them personally. It means that you took the time and made the effort to learn their name.

Know your clients names, know what they want in regards to service and provide that service in the most professional manner. This "tool" is one that is most valuable and only few possess. You will find that it will help you become successful and rich.

Wahl, Andis and Oster all brands of barber clippers that can be relied upon by a competent barber/stylist.

# A Final Word

I put together this little handbook because there are a lot of things that I have observed in my many years practicing barbering that I would consider detrimental. For this reason I felt compelled to share bits of wisdom that I have learned over the years.

For the record, I love this industry of barbering and cosmetology and I have a desire to see it continue to thrive and move forward. I believe that if you take the simple principles that I have laid out in this booklet and apply them as they should be applied you will absolutely be successful and ultimately rich!

The first chapter dealt with the subject of "love" and I cannot emphasize enough how important that is. In the event that you become a shop owner or manager, you will want your shop to be professional, clean and organized. But you will also want it to be an atmosphere that is filled with love. The feeling of love releases endorphins into your brain that cause an overall good and euphoric feeling. When someone has that feeling it is expressed and outwardly begins to permeate the environment of those affected.

If your shop or salon is a loving environment, you will have happy barbers, stylists, owners, managers and most important, clients. That is the ideal workplace and will create the most potential for you to get rich. People are always attracted to places where there is love and laughter so keep your shop full of both while remaining professional.

Another thing that I would like for you to keep in mind is the fact that as a barber/stylist one of your goals should be to grow your business. Growth is a necessary factor if one is to become rich and successful but do not expect for it to come real fast. Growth of any kind should always come in degrees because if you grow to fast in business yet do not have the resources to accommodate it then you end up losing all that you have gained.

Unusually fast growth is an indicator that the growth is neither "real" or "sustainable." What comes to mind is the .com boom of the 1990s. Then you saw a bunch of online companies that were being traded publicly growing exponentially. The problem was that most of them were just "straw" companies that had neither real products or real customers. People were simply coming up with any and every idea they could to get in on the .com craze that was happening at the time.

As a barber or cosmetologist, you are a real, organic business and growth should be facilitated based upon that fact. That means grow in a deliberate fashion that you can afford. Invest in your business as often as you can without going into debt and your growth will be genuine and without unnecessary risk.

Remember, this is practical information and bits of wisdom that I have gained through experience. Most times when one wants to learn something they go to a school, college or university where the professor may or may not have any experience in the field that they are "professing" to teach you. I just gave you the benefit of "real world" experience and compiled it in a small book. Again, I hope and pray that it is helpful.

Peace.

Your barber and author, Herman "SupremeStyle"
Muhammad.

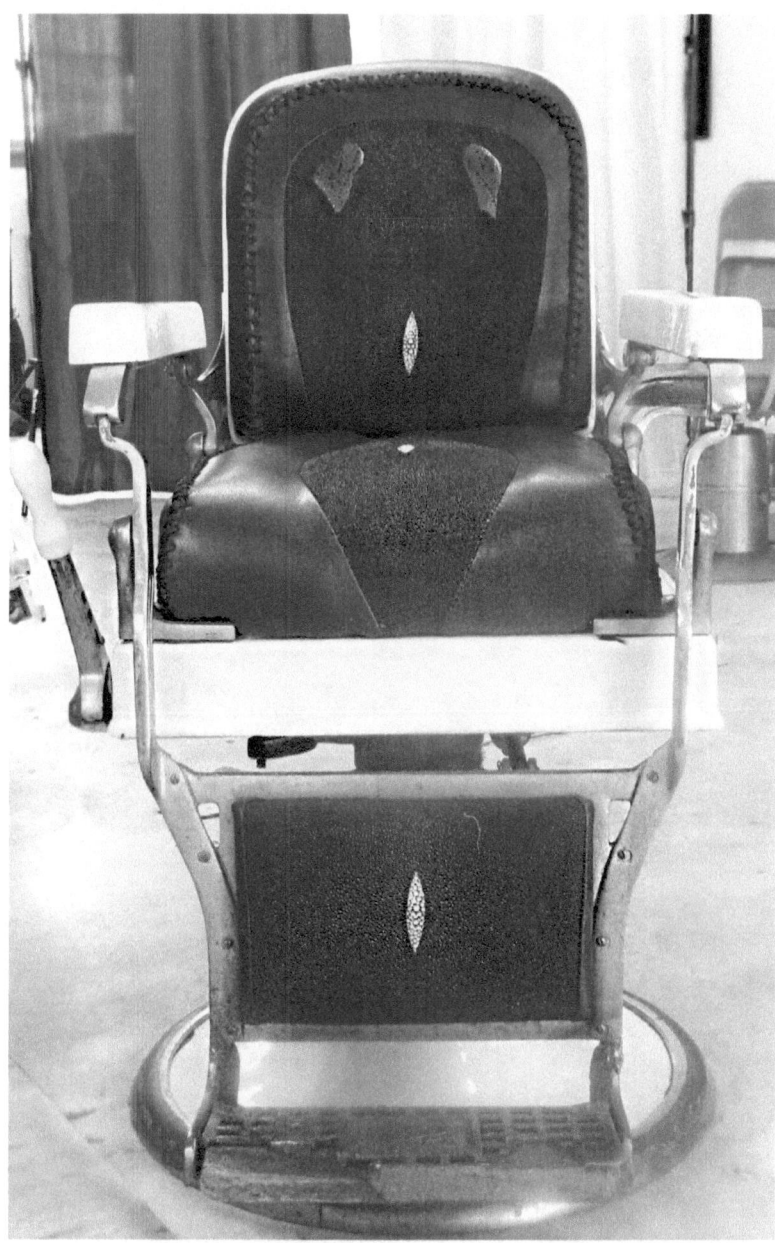

My porcelain barber chair made with quality cowhide, stingray and frog.

A scene from my shop Supreme Style Barbershop.

This ad was one of our most successful....

# Notes: